Get Children Writing

Creative writing exercises for teaching students aged 8–11

Sue Walsh

First published 2023

by John Catt Educational Ltd,
15 Riduna Park, Station Road,
Melton, Woodbridge IP12 1QT

Tel: +44 (0) 1394 389850
Fax: +44 (0) 1394 386893
Email: enquiries@johncatt.com
Website: www.johncatt.com

ISBN: 978 1 915261 74 8

Set and designed by John Catt Educational Limited

Contents

Introduction

After more than twenty years teaching English in primary schools I now work with individuals and small groups of children privately. One of my main aims has always been to improve my students' ability to write both creatively and factually. This is not only a pre-requisite for school but an asset for life.

This book is intended to be used as a resource for the teaching of writing to pupils between the ages of 8 and 11 years (although its exercises could easily be adapted for younger or older pupils).

The twenty-two exercises included are divided into 3 sections: Inspiration, Poetry and References to children's classical literature. I have honed these activities over time and continue to use them myself. They have inspired even my most reluctant students to write, gain confidence and discover their own voice.

Each exercise has clear aims, emphasising learning objectives, aspects of grammar or specific literary techniques. The aims at the start of each chapter are a quick way to identify the most appropriate choice of assignment for a particular class. There are teachers' notes outlining preparation where necessary, although many of these exercises are self-explanatory.

Assignments lead pupils through a series of short questions in the form of notes. Following on, a discussion of ideas and thoughts is encouraged prior to tackling a final piece of writing. Exchanging ideas and hearing others' views enables students to appreciate a wide variety of experiences and interpretations, while at the same time developing their own confidence and sense of self. Examples of work have been included for clarity.

I hope that you enjoy using these exercises with your pupils as much as I have.

A Moment

Aim

1. To focus on the here and now.
2. To develop an understanding of rhythm in our writing.
3. To use the senses.

Assignment

The following simple questions and prompts encourage us to concentrate on each sense. This exercise helps us connect to ourselves and to explore our relationship with our immediate surroundings – the world in which we live and what is happening right now.

These can be answered equally well on a journey – by train, car, or plane – as while sitting in a room at home or in a classroom. However, you will need access to a view through a window.

Answer the following questions and prompts using the present tense:

1. What can you see? Focus on three or four points of interest. Pick out details rather than the generic.

   Staring through the window I see …

2. Stream of consciousness. Allow your thoughts to drift and be sparked by what you see.

   The view reminds me of …

   I am thinking …

3. What can you hear? Make a list of all the sounds around you.

   I can hear …

4. Describe how you feel.

   I feel …

5. Allow your mind to wander. What do you imagine is happening outside?

   Outside I imagine …

Next, we are going to write a poem. Use your notes to write a two- to three-line verse for each point (except for what you can hear). Then, between each verse repeat two or three lines that describe sound.

Read your poem out loud. Listen to it being read by someone else.

Be prepared to alter its lines if they don't sound quite right.

Give your poem a title.

Example:

Dreaming

I am sitting in the lounge,
On a blue settee.
A low table in front
Is piled with books and papers.

The clock ticks,
The blackbird sings.

Staring through the window
I see a house, curtains, two cars, pavement, a driveway,
Plants, a dirty fence,
Some pipes and a lamppost.

The clock ticks,
The blackbird sings.

It reminds me of a gloomy day,
Everyone tucked up warm.

The clock ticks,
The blackbird sings.

I feel as if I am so tired
I could fall asleep.

The clock ticks,
The blackbird sings.

Outside I know my sister is doing
Maths homework.
Mum is shopping.

The clock ticks,
The blackbird sings.

S. J. Walsh

Colour Association

Aim

1. To use the theme of colour to revise basic grammar, i.e. nouns, verbs and adjectives.
2. To understand alliteration and put it into practice.
3. To write creatively by exploring linked associations and new techniques.

Assignment

1. Write down five colours.
2. Beside each colour write your first response or association.
3. Add an adjective, a noun, and a verb.
4. Pick one colour. Using your notes, have a go at writing a sentence using alliteration.

   Alliteration is the repetition of the same sound or letter at the beginning of each or most of the words in a sentence.

5. Use these ideas to form the basis for a short description. It doesn't matter how tenuous your ideas are.

6. Write a short paragraph based on your chosen colour. The notes made earlier can be used or they may trigger a memory, a wish, or a thought that is connected.

Example

Colour	Response	Adjective	Noun	Verb
white	ice	slippery	snow	melting

Alliterative Sentence

I slid across the soft snow; then somersaulted silently down the slope. Swoosh!

Paragraph

I remember skating on ice. It was winter – a grey, blank day. Spiky trees were silhouetted against the sky. The pond had frozen, and I could see my breath like puffs of smoke. We laced up our skates and hobbled to the edge. Pushing off, I glided towards the centre, then half-turned, skating backwards. I could see wide arcs appearing on the surface, my footprints on the ice. There was something exhilarating about skating outside. I felt like a bird floating above the earth. Alive.

Food at Christmas

Aim

1. To practise choosing adjectives carefully to create an accurate image in the mind of the reader or listener.
2. To learn how to personalise a piece of factual writing by including relevant anecdotes or comments.

Assignment

1. Make a list of foods usually associated with the celebration of Christmas. This can be any food connected to Christmas, not just those you eat. You might even choose things you don't particularly enjoy eating.

2. When you have seven to ten items read through them carefully and pick one.

3. Write seven to ten facts about your chosen food without saying what it is.

4.   Write a couple of paragraphs describing your choice of food using the notes you have already made. As you begin, other ideas may come into your mind. Choose what makes for the most interesting reading. Try to personalise your description by including descriptions of the senses – smell, taste, feel and sight.

Example

Food

[Mince Pie]

Facts

- They are made of pastry.
- They have a circular lid.
- I usually make them myself.
- They can be eaten with cream, brandy butter or simply on their own.
- I prefer them warm.
- I like eating them with a cup of tea.
- Inside, there's a mixture of currants, nuts and sultanas.
- You can only buy them in supermarkets around Christmas.
- One would fit into the palm of my hand.

Paragraph

I usually buy several boxes of these from different supermarkets over the Christmas period. Then I compare their taste. Last year my favourites were Tesco 'Finest' and Marks & Spencer basic 'all butter'. The Marks' ones came in a red box and were the cheapest at £1.80 for six. I bought three boxes in total. Every year I intend to make them myself, but I never get round to it. I even buy all the stuff in. The jars and packets are still sitting in my cupboard from last year! Well, let's face it, there's far more interesting things to be doing than standing for an hour or more making pastry and then fiddling around cutting out various sized discs which then need to be eased into trays and filled. If you're really keen you can even make the filling. That's more shopping – currants, sultanas, suet, nuts, etc.

There's something rather comforting in the way the finished item sits neatly in the palm of your hand. I enjoy eating them washed down with a cup of Darjeeling tea. Heaven!

Guess the Present

Aim

1. To write concisely.
2. To select key facts.
3. To use adjectives accurately.

Assignment

1. Make a short list of the gifts you received over Christmas.
2. Select one from your list.
3. Write seven or eight facts about this present, but don't reveal its name. Think about your senses if appropriate – it's appearance, smell, and sound – or what it makes you think of.
4. Write a paragraph describing this present. You may use the notes made in question three. The facts chosen will need to be developed in order to produce a coherent piece of writing. Once you've started,

other thoughts or ideas may come to mind which you may also decide to include.

5. Read your passage aloud to the group or a partner. Then pick someone to guess your present.

Example

[Bubble Bath]

- It comes in a box the shape of a cuboid.
- It is a green liquid.
- It smells of pine trees.
- It looks similar to washing-up liquid.
- You pour a small amount into running water.
- It produces foam.
- You can wallow in it.

The best time to use this is at the end of the day. Pour a couple of capfuls into warm, running water. The smell fills the whole room. Immediately bubbles appear on the surface. More water makes more bubbles. After a few minutes the bubbles become so concentrated they turn into foam. You can no longer see the water. If you drop soap into the bathtub the foam disappears and the water looks like a green sea. When you lie in it you feel as if you are in a dream. I almost fall asleep.

A Point of View: I am a Pencil

Notes for teachers

Place the following inanimate objects in front of the group.

- Pack of playing cards.
- Pencil.
- Small mirror.
- Fork.
- Tin opener.
- Book.
- Key.
- Watch or clock.

Other items may also be chosen for this exercise.

Assignment

1. Pick one of the objects and describe it. Think about its size, shape, use and what it is made from. Mention any fact or connection you feel is relevant. This will be an objective description.

2. Using the second person (using the pronoun 'you') speak to the object as if it is someone you know. Ask questions. It is as if you have formed a relationship.

3. Imagine you are the object. How do you feel? What thoughts pass through your mind? How do you view your life and the future? Think about your irritations, concerns, desires and wishes. Bear in mind your purpose or job. Write a couple of paragraphs from the point of view of the chosen object (use the pronoun 'I').

4. Write a poem based on some of the ideas that have been described in answer to questions two and three. Don't try to include every point. Be selective. Other thoughts may occur to you once you begin, which you may decide to include.

Example one

Description

Here is a pencil. It is exactly 13.2 centimetres long. It has worn away letters with red paint underneath. At the end of the pencil, a red rubber is encased in a metal ring. The lead has been sharpened like a cone.

Second person ('you')

You are under my control. I can make you do anything I choose. I can make you draw, write and sketch. It's up to me to pick you up and drag you across the paper. Would you rather be used a lot or not much?

First person ('I')

I've been dropped down a hill, lost and forgotten. It's starting to get cold. I'm starting to rot. Can you help find me? I've had a life of hard work –

sketching, drawing and writing. I've been getting shorter as my life goes on. Is this the end?

Poem

I am a Pencil

I am a pencil.
I am exactly 13.2 centimetres long.
I have worn away letters,
with red paint underneath.
I have no control –
I get dragged over paper,
whilst getting smaller.
I have been dropped down the hill.
Lost – forgotten,
I am getting cold,
I'm beginning to rot.
I've had a life of hard work;
Sketching, drawing, writing.
Could this be the end?

George Godfrey, aged ten.

Example two

I am a Pack of Cards

I am a pack of cards,
There are fifty-two altogether:
Two to ten, Jack, Queen, King and Ace.
I am four suits,
Hearts, diamonds, clubs and spades.

I am well used,
My corners are bent.
My faces are dirty,
From hands touching me;
Playing endless games.

I am tired
Of being shuffled and dealt.
How long can I keep playing?
Rummy, Stop the Bus and Twenty-ones.
I am a pack of cards.

Isabella Benfield, aged ten.

Let's Look at a Painting

Aim

- To develop observational skills.
- To express our thoughts and feelings and learn to understand them.
- To encourage an interest in paintings.

Notes for teachers

Collect a variety of postcards of work by different artists. Try to select a range of styles and subject matter.

Give the students plenty of time to look at all of them, before choosing one.

Below are some examples of art which I have used to inspire students for this exercise:

David Hockney (b. 1937)	*Nichols Canyon*
	Felled Trees on Woldgate
Chris Ofili (b. 1968)	*Poolside Magic 12*
Georgia O'Keeffe (1887-1986)	*Black Mesa Landscape, New Mexico*
	Jimson Weed/White Flower No. 1
Vincent van Gogh (1853-1890)	*Seascape Near Les Saintes-Maries-de-la-Mer*
	Wheatfield under Thunderclouds

Assignment

Look carefully at the postcards of different paintings.

Choose one.

Write down answers to the following questions:

1. What draws you to this picture?
2. Describe what you see. The images may not be obvious. In that case describe what *you* feel is there.
3. Which colours have been used predominantly?
4. Describe the style. For example, look at the brushstrokes and the use of light and dark.
5. Describe the main focus. What is your eye drawn to? Do you think that this is what the artist intended?
6. Describe the mood. For instance, is this a happy, joyful or sombre picture? Colour and subject matter can help to create mood.
7. Study the background. Describe it. How does this enhance the picture?
8. Having considered the above questions how do you feel about this painting now?
9. Discuss your responses to the above questions.
10. Write the opening of a story inspired by the chosen picture.

Example

Inspired by *Black Mesa Landscape* by Georgia O'Keeffe.

The adventurer Grizzly Griller was trying to find the Abominable Snow Menace. He jumped from a plane, but the wind blew him off course; his parachute caught the top of the trees. He landed heavily.

At first, he felt a bit light-headed, but he got up and headed into the forest, cutting through the leaves with a machete. Then he realised his bag was gone. In the trees above his head, he heard a chattering and squealing. He spotted two monkeys swinging in the branches, then jumping from tree to tree. One of them had his bag. Grizzly waved his arms and shouted. Eventually the monkey dropped his bag. Looking upwards Grizzly thought he saw a movement. He realised this was no monkey but a boy.

Grizzly called out, "What are you doing here?" "I am looking for the Abominable Snow Menace," the boy replied. "My name is Dennis", he said and dropped to the ground. "We might as well join up", said Grizzly.

Grizzly continued through the forest with Dennis following him. Dennis kept asking questions, but Grizzly ignored him. Eventually they came to a desert. It was difficult walking through sand in the heat. They trudged on. Beads of sweat ran down their faces.

Dennis had given up trying to make conversation. Grizzley's back was sore. Eventually they came to an oasis. The water was only shallow but they both fell into it and began to drink. Floating on their backs they could see black mountains in the distance. They both knew that those mountains would be the next challenge. The sky was a brilliant blue. While lying exhausted they spotted a camel in the distance. It too was in search of water. "When that camel kneels down to drink, we could climb on," said Grizzly. "Do you think we can persuade him to get us to the mountains?", said Dennis. Grizzly replied, "Why not?"

The camel padded across the desert with Grizzley and Dennis holding on tight. At times they closed their eyes and slept for a while. Eventually they found themselves at the foot of the Black Mesa Mountains. There was a narrow path leading upwards. Grizzley got a pickaxe out of his bag. They both started the climb. After an hour they stopped to rest. It was then, to the left of the path that they saw the footprint – like a bear's but it was massive. Suddenly, there was a boom! ...

Winston Kelsey, aged 10

Noises

Aim

1. To develop the ability to listen.
2. To write based on sound.

Notes for teachers

It's important that students concentrate on the precise moment and try to eliminate all thoughts about yesterday, later today, tomorrow, in two days' time, etc. It's tricky today with so many distractions – interruption by mobile phones, the lure of online games and the constant updating of social media. Such factors can affect the ability to concentrate.

Before beginning this exercise make sure the classroom environment is conducive to concentration – not too hot or too cold, light but not bright and above all peaceful. The focus is on what we are hearing.

Assignment

1. What do you hear? Listen for three minutes. Then write a list.

2. Now that we are in the moment and focussed let's try again. Close your eyes. Hear those same sounds again. Then allow them to repeat in your head over and over, louder and louder until they transform. Amplify them with your imagination to a point where they become something else, something more dramatic.

3. Take two or three of the above sounds and write down your immediate response. Avoid thinking too hard about it. Write down the first connections that come into your head. It doesn't matter how obscure these ideas are. Simply get them down on paper.

4. Pick one idea and continue to develop it, exploring its many possibilities. The scene is set perhaps – a backdrop for a character, a plot or the beginning of a story. As we write ideas begin to form. Allow your intuition to drive you on. Avoid being over critical or stopping to check or edit. Editing can always be done at a later stage.

Example one

A list of everyday sounds

- A buzzing fly repeatedly hitting the glass window.
- A clock ticking.
- The distant noise of traffic.
- A pigeon cooing.
- The ceiling creaking.
- A pencil scratching on paper.
- The rumble of a train.
- The clank of a construction crane.
- Birds in conversation.
- The ice-cream van's familiar tune.
- The slam of a door.

- Children's voices in the garden next door.

Example two

Imaginatively amplified sounds

- The fly thumps at the glass trying to knock its way through, a prisoner's attempt to break free.
- The rhythm of the clock marks each moment with a deafening click that jars in my head. It is a bomb about to explode.
- The pigeon's distinctive lullaby sends us to sleep and renders us all unconscious.
- Suddenly there is a loud crack above my head. The roof is being torn off.
- Every time my hand moves there's a grating and then a ripping and a tearing of paper as it's being shredded.
- The train thunders past. Metal on metal.
- The burr of traffic is a wave rushing forwards and backwards, backwards and forwards. It is punctuated by clanking metal – an orchestra of mechanical notes, a tuning of parts.
- In the trees, birds compete, first chirping becomes squawking, then the squawking reaches a fever pitch. A flapping of wings whips up the air, altering the frequency. It's an air attack!
- Violent music, and a squeal of brakes announce a tidal wave of ice cream which is flowing down the street!
- A howling wind slams the kitchen door open and shut.
- There are children in the garden but all I can hear is a ringing in my ears.

By leading students along this journey, they can produce surprising work that is unique, engaging and frequently entertaining. This proves my theory that there is a creative voice in all of us.

Example three

Immediate responses

The slam of a door

The door bangs shut. Where? Why? A breeze, a tug of wind. A lilac branch taps at the kitchen window. From it swings an empty bird seed holder. It's swinging manically backwards and forwards like an overreaching pendulum. Paper leaves cling perilously to the tree across the road. Now they're off whipped into the sky – ducking and soaring. The doors upstairs are vibrating. The wind is teasing them, moaning. I can feel it around my ankles. Out of the corner of my eye I see the garden fence rocking and something green skid across the patio. Tiles from a roof are being flipped off, one by one. There's been no warning. Nobody said. This is middle England! The coast is being battered by waves! The boats out at sea are shunted to and fro like bobbins!

The rumble of a train

The rumble of a train entering and then leaving the station reminds me of a trip to the Railway Museum. A bygone era – tons of metal and belching smoke.

Men shovelling coal. Sweat mixed with steam. The ground vibrating under stress. I watch the Blue Pullman pull away from its position beside the other locomotives and burst through hangar-like doors. There's a billowing of steam and smoke. In my mind's eye I catch a glimpse as it reaches the bend and then disappears into the Yorkshire countryside. I'm going to wait to see if the other exhibits start up and make a bid for freedom. Suppose one by one, each engine stirred into life, and began a new journey? A thing of the past meets the future. That would be worth an entrance ticket.

The distant noise of traffic

The distant burr of the traffic, like waves, comes and goes. I expect those who live here have grown accustomed to it and no longer hear it. But the high-pitched clanking of the cranes can't be denied. They are digging deeper into the ground. Holes you could hide in. The area resembles a giant excavation project. More new housing perhaps. Since my family moved here I have heard people talk about the town being ruined by all the new development. I can't see what's wrong with it. We live in a new house. Well, it's fairly new – not brand new. Dad said it was eight years old which is why we didn't get a survey done when we bought it. It's still got another two years guarantee. I don't believe they are building new houses. I think they've found something. The area is all fenced off and I've seen men in those 'all in one' suits carrying square boxes.

Onomatopoeia

Aim

1. To look at onomatopoeia and understand its effect.
2. To use onomatopoeia in writing.

Onomatopoeia is a word that sounds like the noise it is describing. These words create a sound effect that makes descriptions more expressive and interesting.

The following examples have been categorised:

Animal sounds: baa, bark, buzz, cackle, caw, chatter, chirp, cheep, cluck, cock-a-doodle-do, hiss, hee-haw, neigh.

Sounds people make: achoo, belch, bawl, gargle, gasp, giggle, mumble, murmur, mutter, whisper, sniff, snort.

Words related to water: bloop, splash, spray, sprinkle, squirt, drip, drizzle.

Words related to air: flutter, fizz, fwoosh, gasp, hush, shush, swoosh, swish, whiff, whoosh, whizz, whip, whisper.

Words related to collisions: bam, bang, clang, clap, clatter, click, clink, screech, slap, thud, thump.

Onomatopoeia in literature

Old MacDonald

Old MacDonald had a farm,

Ee i ee i o!

And on that farm he had some chickens,

Ee i ee i o!

With a cluck-cluck here,

And a cluck-cluck there,

Here a cluck, there a cluck

Everywhere a cluck-cluck.

Old MacDonald had a farm,

Ee i ee i o!

Hush-a-bye Baby

Hush-a-by baby on the tree-top,

When the wind blows the cradle will rock;

When the bough breaks the cradle will fall,

Down tumbles baby, cradle and all.

Assignment

1. Can you think of any other onomatopoeic words not listed above?
2. Make a list of six words that appeal to you. Explain why.
3. Choose six words from one or more categories and write a short paragraph or poem using these sound-words as inspiration.

Example

drip   **drizzle**   **spray**   **fwoosh**   **whizz**   **whoosh**

From the shelter of my car I am watching the rain drip down the windscreen. Through the drizzle, waves pound the beach, sending spray into the air; fwoosh. Small figures are holding onto kites which flutter and then, as if tugged by the clouds themselves, whizz and whoosh higher and higher.

Places are People,
People are Places

Aim

1. To describe a room accurately.
2. To consider what our possessions reveal about us.

Assignment

The most revealing place of all is the home. If you were in the home of a complete stranger, within a short time you would have a clear picture of the sort of person who lived there. The clues are in their possessions. For example, ornaments, books (or lack of them), pictures and photographs. Then there's the style of furniture, colour scheme and tidiness. A simple glance could easily reveal their interests, job, approximate age or stage in life.

1. Describe your bedroom. Think about the following points and then make notes for each one.

   - How your room is laid out. For example, the bed is opposite a window.
   - Furniture.
   - Objects displayed.
   - Pictures on the wall.
   - The curtains/blinds/duvet cover/floor covering.
   - Books.
   - Games.

This list is just a guide. Include anything you feel is relevant. Add detailed information about the particular items that are important to you.

2. Using your notes write a description of your room.

3. When you have finished read your description to someone who does not know you well. Ask that person to pick out things that the description reveals about you.

Notes for teachers

In a group lesson, the completed descriptions could be shuffled before being handed randomly to students to read out. After each reading the class could attempt to guess the author.

Returning to School after the Summer Holiday

Aim

1. To write a factual account.
2. To examine thoughts and feelings.
3. Selecting material to create interest.

Returning to school after a long holiday (whether after Christmas or in the summer) can often stir up emotions, particularly if this means a change of school or a new school year.

By examining these feelings and the thought processes behind them students learn to understand themselves better. It also provides ideal material for personal writing.

Assignment

Consider the following questions. Jot down a few notes or words for each.

The night before

1. How did you feel? Were you anxious or excited about any aspect?
2. What thoughts passed through your mind? It doesn't matter how random or unconnected these thoughts may be.
3. What did you expect?
4. What preparations did you make? For example: shopping for a new uniform, rugby boots, or stationery, etc.

After the first day

1. Pick two positive aspects about the day.
2. Pick two negative aspects about the day.
3. Choose one or two noteworthy episodes that occurred. These may be amusing or irritating events.
4. On reflection, was the day better or worse than you had imagined?

Using these notes, write a couple of paragraphs describing your return to school. Try to include thoughts and feelings in your writing. This makes for personal writing and sets it apart from other people's work. You don't have to include all the points mentioned, be selective. If other ideas come to mind while you are writing, feel free to include them.

Example

Year 6 is a year a lot of people call the most important year. I agree but for some it's a horrid year. All the annoying people you haven't seen are back and just as annoying. Work is harder by a long way compared to year 5 although you are usually smarter. There are more opportunities but also more responsibilities. There are a lot more clubs you can join and you play contact rugby. One of the biggest disadvantages is that you have more homework. It always feels odd returning to school after the summer because you've been on holiday for six weeks! But then you get into the normal routine and it's fine.

Alex White, aged 10

Spoons

Aim

1. To observe carefully.
2. To consider the precise meaning of words.
3. To practice using adjectives to help create a mental picture.

Notes for teachers

Adjectives are words that describe nouns. This exercise uses objects to prompt observation and description.

Assignment one

1. Pick three different spoons, e.g. a wooden mixing spoon, a plastic salad spoon and a silver-plated table spoon.
2. Place a spoon in front of the students, have them pick it up, and examine it carefully.

3. Write down the adjectives that describe it in a list. Then repeat this with the other two spoons.

4. Read the three different lists of adjectives out loud. Discuss which words are key to identifying each spoon.

5. Adjectives can be divided into categories such as:

Appearance   Feel   Taste   Number   Material   Smell

Fill in the categories with the adjectives compiled.

6. This exercise can be repeated using three postcards of different images – such as a flower, a cake and a forest.

Assignment two

Describe your:

1. Skin.
2. Eyes.
3. Hair.
4. Shoes.

Assignment three

Read the following poem aloud and discuss it. How does it make you feel? What does the author remember about their grandfather? How do they create a mental picture of him?

Grandfather

I remember

His sparse white hair and lean face ...

Creased eyes that twinkled when he laughed,

And sea-worn skin,

Patterned to a latticework of lines.

I remember

His blue-veined, calloused hands,

Long gnarled fingers
Stretching out towards the fire –
Three fingers missing –
Yet he was able to make model yachts,
And weave baskets.
Each bronzed autumn
He would gather berries.
Each breathing spring
His hands were filled with flowers.
I remember
Worshipping his fisherman's yarns,
Watching his absorbed expression
As he solved the daily crossword
With the slim cigarette, hand rolled,
Placed between his lips.
I remember
The snowdrops,
The impersonal hospital bed,
The reek of antiseptic.
I remember, too,
The weeping child
And wilting daffodils
Laid upon his grave.

Susan Hrynkow, aged thirteen.

1. Write a short description of someone you know well – a brother or sister, mother, father, grandma, close friend.
2. Try to pick out the things that stand out for you. Often these are our first thoughts.
3. Draw three things that represent your chosen person.

The Place Where I Live

Aim

1. To write a description.
2. To use adjectives accurately.
3. To be selective in the choice of material included.

Notes for teachers

The questions in assignment one are a guide only. Some may not be appropriate, depending on the place being described.

Assignment one

Whether you live in a city, town, village or in a rural area, picture it in your mind. Think about your immediate surroundings. If you live on a road there may be houses, shops, restaurants, a garage, or a bus stop. In the countryside, think about the changing landscape and patterns in the sky. It may help to imagine that you're looking through a window.

Answer the following questions:

1. How long have you lived there?
2. Are there any distinguishing features, such as a castle, a river or a building of special interest?
3. Is there an area that is considered particularly beautiful? For example, views, walks or squares?
4. Are there any interesting independent shops or restaurants?
5. What people do you know there?
6. In your opinion, would visitors enjoy exploring this area?
7. In the time you've lived there have there been many changes? Explain.

Assignment two

Write a description of where you live. Focus on aspects that interest you and why, as opposed to trying to mention everything. Small details make for a personal account, details that only someone who lives there would know.

Assignment three

Try to imagine what a stranger who's visiting for the first time would immediately notice or want to see. This may be difficult to imagine if we've lived in a place for many years as we tend not to notice things that are overly familiar. It may help to imagine you have a friend coming to stay who is similar in age. Where would you take them?

Write down your ideas.

Who am I?

Aim

1. To understand ourselves.
2. To explore our dreams.
3. To write objectively.

Assignment

How well do we know ourselves?

Answer the following questions to find out!

1. Make a list of the activities you enjoy.
2. If the day was yours to spend as you choose, describe what you would do.
3. What makes you laugh?
4. What makes you angry?

5. Describe an occasion that you either found very amusing or particularly irritating.

6. Do you have a burning ambition to do something or travel somewhere? Explain why.

7. Pick five adjectives that describe you.

8. Reading through your responses to the above questions, how well do you think you know yourself?

9. Using your notes, write a couple of paragraphs about yourself. Start with 'My name is ...'. Choose what you wish to include. Other ideas may come to mind when you're writing, which you may include if you wish.

Notes for teachers

This is a spontaneity exercise. If students struggle to answer any of the questions you can suggest that they miss those out and return to them later. Something may come to mind but if not, they can leave it out. The point of this exercise is to explore oneself.

Question one

Once students have made their lists ask them to read over them and then read them out loud to the group or a partner.

Discuss the list in more detail. For example:

Swimming. Where do you swim, e.g. the local leisure centre, or the sea? What type of swimming do you do, e.g. breast-stroke, butterfly, or crawl? Do you swim for fun or competitively? How often do you do this?

Painting. What kind of things do you like to paint, e.g. still life, landscape or from photographs? What medium do you use?

The aim is to discover precisely which aspects of the activity is enjoyed.

Question two

Students shouldn't include everything listed in question one. Encourage them to be selective. Remember it's only one day. They should choose two or three activities or excursions at the most.

Questions three and four

Specific events or situations can trigger an emotion. Give some examples. If this is proving difficult for students, then ask them to think back to the last time they were angry or laughed. What caused this feeling? Would they feel the same in a similar situation? By answering further questions, they may be able to identify a common thread.

Question five

Ask students to briefly describe an event they remember. It doesn't matter how long ago it was.

Question six

Some children will have little problem answering this while others will have no idea. For those who don't know, they can think it through at their leisure. Often discussing other people's responses can lead us to realisations about ourselves.

Question seven

Reading their notes should provide some accurate descriptions here. This question is asking students to be objective about themselves.

Question eight

This could be the basis of an interesting discussion. For many students there will be aspects of their character that will be a revelation, or that they are only now consciously realising.

POETRY

Colour Poems

Aim

1. To make connections based on a specific colour.
2. To write a poem based on associations.
3. To hone listening skills.

Notes for teachers

Read the following poem out loud to the group.

Discuss what is associated with the colour red. Emphasise sounds and feelings as well as things that can be seen.

What is Red?

Red is a sunset,
Blazy and bright.
Red is feeling brave
With all your might.

Red is a sunburn
Spot on your nose,
Sometimes red
Is a red, red rose.
Red squiggles out
When you cut your hand.
Red is a brick and
A rubber band.
Red is a hotness
You get inside
When you're embarrassed
And want to hide.
Fire-cracker, fire-engine
Fire-flicker red –
And when you're angry
Red runs through your head …
Red is a lipstick,
Red is a shout,
Red is a signal
That says: "Watch out!"
Red is a great big
Rubber ball.
Red is the giant-est
Color of all.
Red is a show-off
No doubt about it –
But can you imagine
Living without it?

Mary O'Neill.

Assignment

1. Listen to the poem *What is Red?* being read out loud.
2. Without looking at the poem, try to write down as many of the associations with red that it mentions as you can.
3. What do you associate with the colour red, that hasn't been mentioned by the poet?
4. Think of a colour. Make a list of as many connections or associations as you can. Remember to include food (e.g. fruit and vegetables), feelings and moods, as well as sights.
5. Use the poem *What is Red?* as a template. Pick an association with your colour from your list. Make that your first line. For the second line make a comment on that association. Continue to pick out associations from the list and add comments until you have completed your poem.

Example

What is Gold?

Gold is money,
Pounds and pence.
Gold is the honey,
That bees store.
Gold is joy
A wonderful feeling.
Gold is buttercups
Growing in the field.
Gold are the stars,
In the dark sky.
Gold are fish,
Swimming in a pond.

Gold is sunshine,
On a hot Summer day.
Gold is lemon in a meringue pie.

By Miia Lord, aged 8 years.

A List Poem

Aim

1. To study the techniques used to write a list poem.
2. To consider the mood evoked.
3. To write a list poem based on personal association.

Notes for teachers

Depending on the students' ability the assignment could be done in pairs first and then discussed as a class. This would provide an opportunity for students to give their own interpretation.

It is important to draw attention to the repetition of the 'ing' sound at the end of the lines and the effect this creates.

Spring

Frost melting,
Green bringing,

Tree budding,

Days lengthening,

Snowdrop drooping,

April showering,

Shoots growing,

Seed planting,

Sun shining,

Easter holidaying,

Flower blossoming,

Daffodil picking,

Caterpillar crawling,

Tadpole wriggling,

Butterfly fluttering,

Blackbird chattering,

Nest building,

Chick hatching,

Lamb playing,

Maypole dancing,

Warm wind whispering.

A. Ingram

The poet has thought about their associations with the season of spring and these ideas have formed the basis for this poem.

Assignment

If possible, do the following exercise in pairs.

1. Read the poem out loud to each other. Listening and speaking are two very different experiences. By doing both you will gain different insights as to the poem's meaning.

2. Pick out lines you particularly like and explain why.

3. Discuss the way the poem has been written and its rhythm.

4. What do you think the following lines mean?

   a. Green bringing.

   b. Blackbird chattering.

   c. Warm wind whispering.

5. Think about Christmas and make a list of your associations with this time of year. Try to make use of the senses – sight, smell, sound – as well as your feelings and thoughts. Doing this makes for more interest and personalises your writing.

6. Using your notes, make up your own list poem about Christmas.

You may decide to make the lines of your poem longer than *Spring*.

Avoid deliberately trying to make a poem rhyme as this can compromise the meaning.

Every so often, pause and read it aloud. Be prepared to change words and/ or lines if it doesn't flow.

Have fun!

Example

Christmas

Nutmeg,
Cinnamon,
Wood burning.
Twinkling lights around the fire.
Through the window
Snow is falling
Like fur.
Snowmen stand in the distance.
Beyond the dining room food is roasting,
Turkey,

Pigs in blankets,
Sprouts.
Pulling crackers,
Watching 'Elf' on television.
Waiting to unwrap
More presents!

Milly, aged ten.

Ode to a Room

Assignment

An ode is an address or homage to a particular subject.

Look around the room you are in.

1. Make a list of seven things (common nouns); they could be items of furniture, ornaments or pictures. Choose things that catch your attention or interest you.

2. Choose an adjective to describe each noun and write it down next to the object.

3. Look carefully at each chosen object and choose another adjective. Read carefully through your list of nouns and adjectives.

4. Write a fact or observation about each noun in the form of one or two sentences. You may decide to include some or all of the adjectives. Or they may simply act as a prompt. It is your choice.

5. Using the notes that you've made, write an ode to the room you are in. Set it out as a poem. Begin each line with a capital letter. Other thoughts and ideas may come to mind as you begin, which you may also decide to include.

6. Think of an interesting final line as a conclusion.

Example

Dining Room

List of nouns and adjectives

Table – oak – dented

Chair – hard – upright

Fireplace – brick – dusty

Couch – worn – old

Picture – faded – pale

Clock – carriage – noisy

Rug – woven – rippled

Observations

The oak table is marked and dented. It belonged to my Grandma.

There are six chairs, hard and upright.

The red, brick fireplace is boarded up. I can't remember when or if a fire has ever been lit in it.

The old couch sags in the middle but is as comfortable as a bed.

A picture of sheep grazing in a field is the same view as from the window.

The carriage clock ticks noisily – a wedding present to my parents.

Beneath my feet I can feel the ripples of the rug like mountains and valleys before me.

Ode to a Dining Room

There is an old oak table in the centre.

I am leaning on it.

Six chairs, hard and upright fit tightly underneath.

Opposite the brick fireplace gathers dust.

The couch – worn and sagging reminds me of a favourite jumper.

Beneath my feet I feel the rug's ripples,

Mountains and valleys.

Sheep graze in a field in a picture on the wall.

The carriage clock marks time aloud,

Outside the sky darkens.

George Godfrey, aged ten.

Personification in Poetry

Aim

1. To look at the use of personification in poetry.
2. To practise using personification in our own writing.

Personification is when objects or animals are given human qualities, for example, feelings, thoughts or actions. It's a literary tool that adds interest or understanding to a poem or piece or story.

Assignment one

Read the following poem about autumn.

Autumn

As summer draws its final breath,
To prepare its curtain call,
The monarchs begin their epic trek,
To usher in the fall.

The northern wind breathes out its chill,

As songs begin to hush,

And paints the trees upon the hill,

With its artist's brush.

From green to red, orange and brown,

The trees discard their masks,

And lay them gently upon the ground,

For us to begin our tasks.

Autumn makes way for winter's reign,

We bid farewell old friend,

Till summer's warmth begins to wane,

and fall returns again.

Brian C. Kelley

1. With a partner/group discuss how personification is used in the first verse.
2. Think about the phrases: 'final breath', 'curtain call', and 'epic trek'. What are the qualities associated with these descriptions and what kind of images are conjured up as a result?
3. The writer's tone or voice can pervade a text with joy, anxiety, anger, celebration or gloom. Different elements of writing can help to create this. The first verse sets the mood or tone of the poem. What is the mood in this case? Give reasons for your answer.
4. In verse two the trees begin to change colour. Explain how the poet conveys this.
5. In verse three, 'the trees discard their masks and lay them gently upon , the ground'. What does this line mean?
6. Read verse four. Describe the feeling evoked. How is this achieved?

Notes for teachers

The following are some points worth discussing when answering the questions in assignment one.

Questions one and two

There are several examples of personification

- 'final breath' (death/end of life)
- 'curtain call' (end of a play/final bow)
- 'epic trek' (long journey)

Question three

Melancholy and/or sadness is suggested by the phrases 'final breath' and 'curtain call'.

Question four

In verse two it is as if an artist has painted the leaves different colours.

Question five

In verse three this metaphor means that the trees are losing their leaves, the leaves being like masks that hide the trees' shape. Shape could refer to identity.

Question six

The end of the poem is hopeful. Although we're saying goodbye to autumn it will return.

Assignment two

We are going to dream up our own personification.

1. Pick a season: autumn, winter, spring or summer. Then make a list of associations with that particular time of year. It's worth reading the list poem *Spring* (pp. 57-58) for ideas.

2. Make a list of ten to fifteen action words (verbs) that name things humans engage in, for example, run, cry, whisper, laugh and so on. Beside each seasonal phrase you've chosen (see question one), imagine a human action that conjures up that image. You can use a verb from the list you have just written or you may think of new action words.

There's no right or wrong. Let you imagination take over. The purpose is to enhance your writing by creating a vivid picture.

3. Taking each line extend your ideas. Create a verse for each one until you have a poem. Give it a title.

Example

Season

Winter

Seasonal phrase	action word
Dark days	struggle
Bare trees	shiver
Frozen paths	invite
Our breath	belch
Blank sky	moans
Winter sun	smiles

Winter

Dark days cut short,
Struggle on.

Trees stand naked,
Shivering.

Frozen paths,
An invitation.

Our breath belches
Warm clouds.

The blank sky
Moans.

Occasionally,
Sun smiles at us.

Extracts from Children's Classics

Other Worlds: *The Lion, the Witch and the Wardrobe* and *Alice in Wonderland*

Aim

1. To identify the use of literary techniques.
2. To practise using these techniques in our writing.
3. To use extracts from well-known classics as a springboard for creative writing.

Extracts

Read the following two extracts. They both describe fictional characters entering strange other worlds.

The Lion, the Witch and the Wardrobe by C. S. Lewis

Chapter one – Lucy looks into the wardrobe

Once there were four children whose names were Peter, Susan, Edmund, and Lucy. This story is about something that happened to them when they were sent away from London during the war because of the air-raids. They were sent to the house of an old Professor who lived in the heart of the country, ten miles from the nearest railway station and two miles from the nearest post office. He had no wife and he lived in a very large house with a housekeeper named Mrs Macready and three servants ... He himself was a very old man with shaggy white hair which grew over much of his face as well as on his head, and they liked him almost at once; but on the first evening when he came out to meet them at the front door he was so odd-looking that Lucy (who was the youngest) was a little afraid of him, and Edmund (who was the next youngest) wanted to laugh and had to keep on pretending he was blowing his nose to hide it.

As soon as they had said goodnight to the Professor and gone upstairs on the first night, the boys came into the girls' room and they all talked it over ...

... when the next morning came there was a steady rain falling, so thick that when you looked out of the window you could see neither the mountains nor the woods nor even the stream in the garden.

"Of course it *would* be raining!" said Edmund. They had just finished breakfast with the Professor and were upstairs in the room he had set apart for them – a long, low room with two windows looking in one direction and two in another.

"Do stop grumbling, Ed," said Susan. "Ten to one it'll clear up in an hour or so. And in the meantime we're pretty well off. There's a wireless and lots of books."

"Not for me," said Peter, "I'm going to explore in the house."

Everyone agreed to this, and that was how the adventures began. It was the sort of house you never seem to come to the end of, and it was full of unexpected places. The first few doors they tried led only into spare bedrooms, as everyone had expected that they would; but soon they came to a very long room full of pictures, and there they found a suit of armour; and after that was a room all hung with green, with a harp in one corner; and then came three steps down and five steps up, and then a kind of little upstairs hall and a door that led out onto a balcony, and then a whole series of rooms that led into each other and were lined with books – most of them very old books and some bigger than a Bible in a church. And shortly after that they looked into a room that was quite empty except for one big wardrobe; the sort that has a looking glass in the door. There was nothing else in the room at all except a dead bluebottle on the window-sill.

"Nothing there!" said Peter, and they all trooped out again – all except Lucy. She stayed behind because she thought it would be worthwhile trying the door of the wardrobe, even though she felt almost sure that it would be locked. To her surprise it opened quite easily, and two moth-balls dropped out.

Looking into the inside, she saw several coats hanging up – mostly long fur coats. There was nothing Lucy liked so much as the smell and feel of fur. She immediately stepped into the wardrobe and got in among the coats and rubbed her face against them, leaving the door open, of course, because she knew that it is very foolish to shut oneself into any wardrobe. Soon she went further in and found that there was a second row of coats hanging up behind the first one. It was almost quite dark in there and she kept her arms stretched out in front of her so as not to bump her face into the back of the wardrobe. She took a step further in – then two or three steps – always expecting to feel woodwork against the tips of her fingers. But she could not feel it.

"This must be a simply enormous wardrobe!" thought Lucy, going still further in and pushing the soft folds of the coats aside to make room for her. Then she noticed that there was something crunching under her feet. "I wonder is that more mothballs?" she thought, stooping down to feel it with her hand. But instead of feeling the hard, smooth wood of the floor of the wardrobe, she felt something soft and powdery and extremely cold. "This is very queer," she said, and went on a step or two further.

Next moment she found that what was rubbing against her face and hands was no longer soft fur but something hard and rough and even prickly. "Why, it is just like branches of trees!" exclaimed Lucy. And then she saw that there was a light ahead of her; not a few inches away where the back of the wardrobe ought to have been, but a long way off. Something cold and soft was falling on her. A moment later she found that she was standing in the middle of a wood at night-time with snow under her feet and snowflakes falling through the air.

Lucy felt a little frightened, but she felt very inquisitive and excited as well. She looked back over her shoulder and there, between the dark tree trunks, she could still see the open doorway of the wardrobe and even catch a glimpse of the empty room from which she had set out. (She had, of course, left the door open, for she knew that it is a very silly thing to shut oneself into a wardrobe.) It seemed to be still daylight there. "I can always get back if anything goes wrong," thought Lucy. She began to walk forward, *crunch- crunch*, over the snow and through the wood towards the other light.

In about ten minutes she reached it and found it was a lamp-post. As she stood looking at it, wondering why there was a lamp-post in the middle of a wood and wondering what to do next, she heard a pitter patter of feet coming towards her. And soon after that a very strange person stepped out from among the trees into the light of the lamp-post.

He was only a little taller than Lucy herself and he carried over his head an umbrella, white with snow. From the waist upwards he was like a man, but his legs were shaped like a goat's (the hair on them was glossy black) and instead of feet he had goat's hoofs. He also had a tail, but Lucy did not notice this at first because it was neatly caught up over the arm that held the umbrella so as to keep it from trailing in the snow. He had a red woollen muffler round his neck and his skin was rather reddish too. He had a strange, but pleasant little face with a short pointed beard and curly hair, and out of the hair there stuck two horns, one on each side of his forehead. One of his hands, as I have said, held the umbrella: in the other arm he carried several brown-paper parcels. What with the parcels and the snow it looked just as if he had been doing his Christmas shopping. He was a Faun. And when he saw Lucy he gave such a start of surprise that he dropped all his parcels.

"Goodness gracious me!" exclaimed the Faun.

Alice's Adventures in Wonderland by Lewis Carroll

Chapter one – Down the rabbit-hole

Alice was beginning to get very tired of sitting by her sister on the bank, and of having nothing to do: once or twice she had peeped into the book her sister was reading, but it had no pictures or conversations in it, "and what is the use of a book," thought Alice, "without pictures or conversations?"

So she was considering in her own mind (as well as she could, for the hot day made her feel very sleepy and stupid), whether the pleasure of making a daisy-chain would be worth the trouble of getting up and picking the daisies, when suddenly a White Rabbit with pink eyes ran close by her.

There was nothing so very remarkable in that; nor did Alice think it so very much out of the way to hear the Rabbit say to itself, "Oh dear! Oh dear! I shall be late!" (when she thought it over afterwards, it occurred to her that she ought to have wondered at this, but at the time it all seemed quite natural); but, when the Rabbit actually *took a watch out of its waistcoat-pocket*, and looked at it, and then hurried on, Alice started to her feet, for it flashed across her mind that she had never before seen a rabbit with either a waistcoat-pocket, or a watch to take out of it, and burning with curiosity, she ran across the field after it, and was just in time to see it pop down a large rabbit-hole under the hedge.

In another moment down went Alice after it, never once considering how in the world she was to get out again.

The rabbit-hole went straight on like a tunnel for some way, and then dipped suddenly down, so suddenly that Alice had not a moment to think about stopping herself before she found herself falling down what seemed to be a very deep well.

Either the well was very deep, or she fell very slowly, for she had plenty of time as she went down to look about her, and to wonder what was going to happen next. First, she tried to look down and make out what she was coming to, but it was too dark to see anything; then she looked at the sides of the well, and noticed that they were filled with cupboards and book-shelves; here and there she saw maps and pictures hung upon pegs. She took down a jar from one of the shelves as she passed; it was labelled "ORANGE MARMALADE", but to her great disappointment it was empty: she did not like to drop the jar, for fear of killing somebody underneath, so managed to put it into one of the cupboards as she fell past it.

"Well!" thought Alice to herself, "after such a fall as this, I shall think nothing of tumbling down stairs! How brave they'll all think me at home! Why, I wouldn't say anything about it, even if I fell off the top of the house!" (Which was very likely true.)

Down, down, down. Would the fall never come to an end? "I wonder how many miles I've fallen by this time?" she said aloud. "I must be getting somewhere near the centre of the earth. Let me see: that would be four thousand miles down, I think –" (for, you see, Alice had learnt several things of this sort in her lessons in the schoolroom, and though this was not a very good opportunity for showing off her knowledge, as there was no one to listen to her, still it was good practice to say it over) "– yes that's about the right distance – but then I wonder what Latitude or Longitude I've got to?" (Alice had not the slightest idea what Latitude was, or Longitude either, but she thought they were nice grand words to say.)

Presently she began again. "I wonder if I shall fall right *through* the earth! How funny it'll seem to come out among the people that walk with their heads downwards! The Antipathies, I think –" (she was rather glad there *was* no one listening, this time, as it didn't sound at all the right word) "– but I shall have to ask them what the name of the country is, you know. Please, Ma'am, is this New Zealand or Australia?" (and she tried to curtsey as she spoke – fancy *curtseying* as you're falling through the air! Do you think you could manage it?) "And what an ignorant little girl she'll think me for asking! No, it'll never do to ask: perhaps I shall see it written up somewhere."

Down, down, down …

Alice was not a bit hurt, and she jumped up on to her feet in a moment: she looked up, but it was all dark overhead; before her was another long passage, and the White Rabbit was still in sight, hurrying down it. There was not a moment to be lost: away went Alice like the wind, and was just in time to hear it say, as it turned a corner, "Oh my ears and whiskers, how late it's getting!" She was close behind it when she turned the corner, but the Rabbit was no longer to be seen: she found herself in a long, low hall, which was lit up by a row of lamps hanging from the roof.

There were doors all around the hall, but they were all locked; and when Alice had been all the way down one side and up the other, trying every door, she walked sadly down the middle, wondering how she was ever to get out again.

Suddenly she came upon a little three-legged table, all made of solid glass; there was nothing on it except a tiny golden key, and Alice's first thought was that it might belong to one of the doors of the hall; but, alas! either the locks were too large, or the key was too small, but at any rate it would not open any of them. However, on the second time round, she came upon a low curtain she had not noticed before, and behind it was a little door about fifteen inches high: she tried the little golden key in the lock, and to her great delight it fitted!

Assignment

Discuss the following:

1. Compare the setting in which the two extracts begin.
2. Highlight examples in both passages where the senses are described – thoughts, feelings, smell, sight, and touch. What effect does this have?
3. How do Lucy and Alice each enter a strange new world?
4. Look at the opening description of the each 'world'. The reader is able to gain a vivid mental picture. How is this achieved?
5. What literary techniques have been used to help bring these stories to life?

Notes for teachers

Ideally students should be given a copy of the extracts so they can annotate and highlight relevant sections.

Question one

The characters in *The Lion, the Witch and the Wardrobe* were exploring an old house when Lucy stumbles across a magical wardrobe.

Alice was bored and sitting beside her sister who was reading a book.

Both of these situations are plausible and therefore convincing.

Question two

The description of the protagonists' thoughts and feelings help the reader to identify with them and give an insight into their character. This makes them seem real.

Question three

Lucy discovers Narnia through the back of the wardrobe.

Alice follows the White Rabbit into a hole and then finds herself falling before eventually landing.

Question four

'... instead of feeling the hard, smooth wood of the floor of the wardrobe, [Lucy] felt something soft and powdery and extremely cold ... Next moment she found what was rubbing against her face and hands was no longer soft fur but something hard and rough and even prickly.'

'The rabbit- hole went straight on like a tunnel for some way, and then dipped suddenly down, so suddenly that Alice had not a moment to think about stopping herself before she found herself falling down what seemed to be a very deep well. Either the well was very deep, or she fell very slowly, for she had plenty of time as she went down to look about her, and to wonder what was going to happen next.'

Question five

- Interior monologue.
- Direct speech.
- Alliteration.
- Repetition.

Written work

The excerpts we have studied are going to be used as a basic template for your own creative writing.

Bear in mind the following points:

1. Set your story in a place you know well and can describe in such a way that the reader will be able to visualise the setting.

2. Introduce the characters. They need to seem real – with their own thoughts and feelings – and able to observe the situation they find themselves in.

3. Think about how your character/characters will enter a new world. Describe their journey.

4. Once in this new world or environment what happens next? How will your story evolve?

   a. Is there a dilemma that the protagonist has to overcome?

   b. What about the introduction of new characters?

5. Make use of some of the literary techniques we have studied in order to make your story convincing and interesting to read.

6. How will it end?

   a. Try to surprise the reader. Avoid the expected or predictable.

   b. Allow your imagination to run!

Chain of Life: *A Christmas Carol*

Aim

1. To practise writing based on fact.
2. To use memories to write autobiographically.
3. To include reflection in the summary.

A Christmas Carol by Charles Dickens

For primary-aged students the Ladybird Children's Classics abridged version is probably more suitable.

In this section the main character, Scrooge, is visited by the ghost of Marley – his old business partner who has died seven years previously.

Chapter one – Marley's Ghost

As [Scrooge] threw his head back in the chair, his glance happened to rest upon a bell, a disused bell, that hung in the room, and communicated for some purpose now forgotten with a chamber in the highest storey of the building. It was with great astonishment, and with a strange, inexplicable dread, that as he looked, he saw this bell begin to swing. It swung so softly in the outset that it scarcely made a sound; but soon it rang out loudly, and so did every bell in the house.

This might have lasted half a minute, or a minute, but it seemed an hour. The bells ceased as they had begun, together. They were succeeded by a clanking noise, deep down below; as if some person were dragging a heavy chain over the casks in the wine-merchant's cellar. Scrooge then remembered to have heard that ghosts in haunted houses were described as dragging chains.

The cellar-door flew open with a booming sound, and then he heard the noise much louder, on the floors below; then coming up the stairs; then coming straight towards his door.

"It's humbug still!" said Scrooge. "I won't believe it."

His colour changed though, when, without a pause, it came on through the heavy door, and passed into the room before his eyes. Upon its coming in, the dying flame leaped up, as though it cried "I know him; Marley's Ghost!" and fell again.

The same face: the very same. Marley in his pigtail, usual waistcoat, tights and boots; the tassels on the latter bristling, like his pigtail, and his coat-skirts, and the hair upon his head. The chain he drew was clasped about his middle. It was long, and wound round him like a tail; and it was made (for Scrooge observed it closely) of cash-boxes, keys, padlocks, ledgers, deeds and heavy purses wrought in steel. His body was transparent; so that Scrooge, observing him, and looking though his waistcoat, could see the two buttons on his coat behind.

Scrooge had often heard it said that that Marley had no bowels, but he had never believed it until now.

No, nor did he believe it even now. Though he looked the phantom through and through, and saw it standing before him; though he felt the chilling influence of its death-cold eyes; and marked the very texture of the folded kerchief bound about its head and chin, which wrapper he had not observed before; he was still incredulous, and fought against his senses.

"How now!" said Scrooge, caustic and cold as ever. "What do you want with me?" ...

"... why do spirits walk the earth, and why do they come to me?"

"It is required of every man," the Ghost returned, "that the spirit within him should walk abroad among his fellow men, and travel far and wide; and if that spirit goes not forth in life, it is condemned to do so after death. It is doomed to wander through the world – oh, woe is me! – and witness what it cannot share, but might have shared on earth, and turned to happiness!"

Again the spectre raised a cry, and shook its chain and wrung its shadowy hands.

"You are fettered," said Scrooge, trembling. "Tell me why?"

"I wear the chain I forged in life," replied the Ghost. "I made it link by link, and yard by yard; I girded it on of my own free will, and of my own free will I wore it. Is its pattern strange to you?"

Scrooge trembled more and more.

"Or would you know," pursued the Ghost, "the weight and length of the strong coil you bear yourself? It was full as heavy and as long as this, seven Christmas Eves ago. You have laboured on it, since. It is a ponderous chain!"

Scrooge glanced about him on the floor, in the expectation of finding himself surrounded by some fifty or sixty fathoms of iron cable: but he could see nothing.

Assignment

If you too had a 'chain of life', what would it be made of? Think of key events that have occurred in your past that may form the links of this chain.

Try not to over think. There may be events that immediately spring to mind that you can picture as if they happened yesterday. Although Marley's chain is forged of regrets and meanness, your own might be associated with happy or sad moments. For example, you might include a particular birthday, a celebration, the first time you visited somewhere or met a significant person.

1. Make a list of key events in your life. Jot these down as you recall them.

2. Now put these events in chronological order.

3. Pick out one event you remember clearly. In a short paragraph describe this in more detail.

4. Why did you pick this event? In what way do you think this has affected you?

Characters in Action:
Wind in the Willows

Aim

1. To explore the different ways in which characters reveal their personality.
2. To use mind maps to record our findings.
3. To widen vocabulary.

Wind in the Willows by Kenneth Grahame

Mole meets the Water Rat for the first time

As [Mole] sat on the grass and looked across the river, a dark hole in the bank opposite, just above the water's edge, caught his eye, and dreamily he fell to considering what a nice snug dwelling-place it would make for an animal with few wants and fond of a **bijou** riverside residence, above flood level and **remote** from noise and dust. As he gazed, something bright and small seemed to twinkle down in the heart of it, vanished, then twinkled once more like a tiny star. But it could hardly be a star in such an unlikely situation; and it was too glittering and small for a glow-worm. Then, as he looked, it winked at him, and so declared itself to be an eye; and a small face began gradually to grow up round it, like a frame round a picture.

A brown little face, with whiskers.

A grave round face, with the same twinkle in its eye that had first attracted his notice.

Small neat ears and thick silky hair.

It was the Water Rat!

Then the two animals stood and regarded each other cautiously.

"Hullo, Mole!" said the Water Rat.

"Hullo, Rat!" said the Mole.

"Would you like to come over?" enquired the Rat presently.

"Oh, it's all very well to *talk*," said the Mole, rather **pettishly** he being new to a river and riverside life and its ways.

The rat said nothing, but stooped and unfastened a rope and hauled on it; then lightly stepped into a little boat which the Mole had not observed. It was painted blue outside and white within, and was just the size for two animals; and the Mole's whole heart went out to it at once, even though he did not fully understand its uses.

The Rat **sculled** smartly across and made fast. Then he held up his **forepaw** as the Mole stepped **gingerly** down. "Lean on that!" he said. "Now then, step lively!" and the Mole to his surprise and rapture found himself actually seated in the **stern** of a real boat.

"This has been a wonderful day!" said he, as the Rat shoved off and took to the sculls again. "Do you know, I've never been in a boat before in all my life."

"What?" cried the Rat, open-mouthed: "Never been in a – you never – well I –what have you been doing, then?"

"Is it so nice as all that?" asked the Mole shyly, though he was quite prepared to believe it as he leant back in his seat and **surveyed** the cushions, the oars, the rowlocks, and all the fascinating fittings, and felt the boat sway lightly under him.

"Nice? It's the only thing," said the Water Rat solemnly, as he leant forward for his stroke. "Believe me, my young friend, there is *nothing* – absolutely nothing – half so much worth doing as simply messing about in boats. Simply messing," he went on dreamily: "messing – about – in – boats; messing – –"

"Look ahead, Rat!" cried the Mole suddenly.

It was too late. The boat struck the bank full tilt. The dreamer, the joyous oarsman, lay on his back at the bottom of the boat, his heels in the air.

"– about in boats – or *with* boats," the Rat went on composedly, picking himself up with a pleasant laugh. "In or out of 'em, it doesn't matter. Nothing seems really to matter, that's the charm of it. Whether you get away, or … you never get anywhere at all, you're always busy, and you never do anything in particular; and when you've done it there's always something else to do, and you can do it if you like, but you'd much better not. Look here! If you've really nothing else on hand this morning, supposing we drop down the river together, and have a long day of it?"

The Mole waggled his toes from sheer happiness, spread his chest with a sigh of full contentment, and leaned back blissfully into the soft cushions. "*What* a day I'm having!" he said. "Let us start at once!"

"Hold hard a minute, then!" said the Rat. He **looped the painter** through a ring in his landing-stage, climbed up into his hole above, and after a short interval reappeared staggering under a fat, wicker **luncheon-basket**.

"Shove that under your feet," he observed to the Mole, as he passed it down into the boat. Then he untied the painter and took the sculls again.

"What's inside it?" asked the Mole, wriggling with curiosity.

"There's cold chicken inside it," the Rat replied briefly;

"**coldtonguecoldhamcoldbeefpickledgherkinssaladfrenchrolls cresssandwidchespottedmeatgingerbeerlemonadesodawater – –**"

"O stop, stop," cried the Mole in **ecstasies**: "This is too much!"

"Do you really think so?" enquired the Rat seriously. "It's only what I always take on these little excursions; and the other animals are always telling me that I'm a mean beast and cut it *very* fine!"

The Mole never heard a word he was saying. Absorbed in the new life he was entering upon, intoxicated with the sparkle, the ripple, the scents and the sounds and the sunlight, he trailed a paw in the water and dreamed long waking dreams …

The Water Rat and Mole join Toad on an excursion.

When they were quite ready, the now triumphant Toad led his companions to the paddock and set them to capture the old grey horse, who without having been consulted, and to his own extreme annoyance, had been told off by Toad for the dustiest job in this dusty expedition. He frankly preferred the paddock, and took a great deal of catching. Meantime Toad packed the lockers still tighter with necessaries, and hung **nose-bags**, nets of onions, bundles of hay, and baskets from the bottom of the cart. At last the horse was caught and harnessed, and they set off, all talking at once, each animal either trudging by the side of the cart or sitting on the shaft, as the humour took him. It was a golden afternoon. The smell of the dust they kicked up was rich and satisfying; out of thick orchards on either side of the road, birds called and whistled to them cheerily; good-natured wayfarers, passing them, gave them "Good day," or stopped to say nice things about their beautiful cart; and rabbits, sitting at their front doors in the hedgerows, held up their fore-paws and said, "O my! O my! O my!"

Late in the evening, tired and happy and miles from home, they drew up on a remote common far from habitations, turned the horse loose to graze, and ate their simple supper sitting on the grass by the side of the cart. Toad **talked big** about all he was going to do in the days to come, while stars grew fuller and larger all around them, and a yellow moon, appearing suddenly and silently from nowhere in particular, came to keep them company and listen to their talk. At last they turned in to their little bunks in the cart; and Toad, kicking out his legs, sleepily said, "Well, good night, you fellows! This is the real life for a gentleman! Talk about your old river!"

"I *don't* talk about my river," replied the patient Rat. "You *know* I don't, Toad. But I *think* about it," he added **pathetically**, in a lower tone: "I *think* about it – all the time!'

The Mole reached out from under his blanket, felt for the Rat's paw in the darkness, and gave it a squeeze. "I'll do whatever you like, Ratty," he whispered. "Shall we run away tomorrow morning, quite early – *very* early – and go back to our dear old hole on the river?"

"No, no, we'll see it out," whispered back the Rat. "Thanks awfully, but I ought to stick by Toad till this trip is ended. It wouldn't be safe for him to be left to himself. It won't take very long. His **fads** never do. Good night!"

The end was indeed nearer than even the Rat suspected.

After so much open air and excitement the Toad slept very soundly, and no amount of shaking could rouse him out of bed next morning. So the Mole and Rat turned to, quietly and manfully, and while the Rat saw to the horse, and lit a fire, and cleaned last night's cups and platters, and got things ready for breakfast, the Mole trudged off to the nearest village, a long way off, for milk and eggs and various necessaries the Toad had, of course, forgotten to provide. The hard work had all been done, and the two animals were resting, thoroughly exhausted by

> the time Toad appeared on the scene, fresh and gay, remarking what a pleasant easy life it was they were all leading now, after the cares and worries and **fatigues of housekeeping** at home.

Assignment

What can we learn about the three characters from these extracts? Consider how each character behaves (**actions**), what they say in conversations (**dialogue**), and the comments characters make about each other (**inferences**). What do these points tell us about their personalities?

1. Read the extracts and discuss the highlighted vocabulary (see notes).
2. Have students reread extract one and make a note of each action, dialogue, or inference that reveals the characters of the Mole and the Water Rat. Alternatively, give each student a copy of the extract and have them highlight each point – e.g. green for action, yellow for dialogue, and blue for inferences etc.
3. Make a mind map for each character (see notes).
4. Using your notes write a description of each of these two characters.
5. What can we learn about Toad from extract two? Make a mind map of his characteristics.
6. Does extract two reveal any further qualities of the Rat and Mole? Describe what these are.

Notes for teachers

Vocabulary

Discuss the following vocabulary.

Extract one: bijou, remote, pettishly, sculled, forepaw, stern, surveyed, 'he looped the painter', luncheon-basket, ecstasies, and 'coldtonguecoldhamcoldbeefpickledgherkinssaladfrenchrollscressand widgespottedmeatgingerbeerlemonadesodawater'.

Extract two: nose-bags, 'talked big', pathetically [i.e. as in pathos, rather than abjectly], fads, and 'fatigues of house-keeping'.

Examples

Mind map: Mole

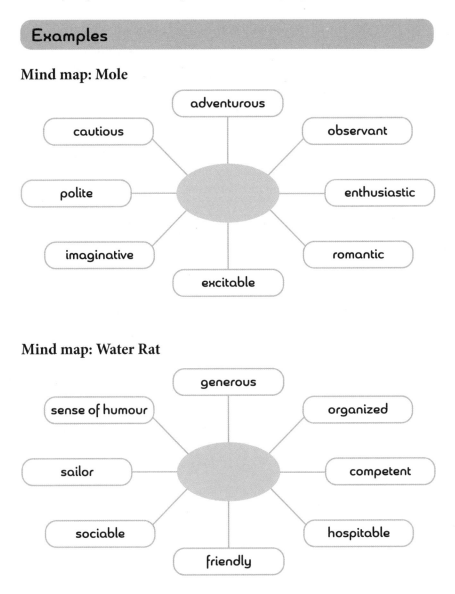

Mind map: Water Rat

Notes on Mole and Rat

Mole

Mole is an observant creature who notices that buried in the bank opposite is an eye. It is the eye of a Water Rat. Both creatures are initially cautious when they first meet. After greeting each other politely the Rat invites Mole to come over. "'Oh, it's all very well to *talk*," said Mole pettishly he being new to a river ...'. The line shows Mole is irritated because he is new to the river and cannot possibly see how he could cross to the other side. However, his adventurous side is shown when he takes up the offer of a ride in the Rat's boat. To his surprise he finds himself thoroughly enjoying the experience – the sway of the boat and 'the fascinating fittings' (i.e. the soft cushions). This description implies he has an imaginative and romantic nature.

When the Rat describes what is in the picnic Mole is ecstatic which suggests his love of food. The final sentence describes Mole as entering a dream-like state as he wallows in this new life on the river.

Rat

The Water Rat is a friendly creature who invites Mole over on their first meeting. He demonstrates confidence and experience as a sailor when he collects Mole from the other side of the riverbank in his boat. Despite this he is prone to dream as the boat later hits the bank and sends him flying. This he finds funny. The Rat loves river life and is shocked to discover that this is Mole's first and only experience in a boat. He is keen to show Mole more and invites him to continue down river. The enormous picnic he prepares to bring along is an example of his generous and sociable nature.

Mind map: Toad

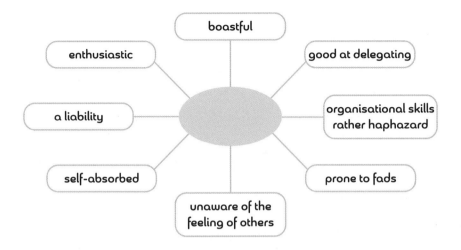

Further characteristics of Mole and Rat

Mole and the Water Rat are both shown to be hard working. Initially they capture the horse who is very reluctant to leave his paddock. This suggests it was not an easy task. The next morning while Toad sleeps, Rat sees to the horse, lights the fire and clears up plates and cups from the night before while Mole trudges to the nearest village for food. Rat is homesick for his life on the river. Mole is very supportive and gives Rat's paw a squeeze and suggests they could run away early in the morning. However, despite his sadness the Water Rat is loyal to Toad and feels responsible for him. This is shown when he replies "No, no, we'll see it out." And "It wouldn't be safe for him to be left to himself."

The passage emphasises the wonderful friendship and support that has developed between Mole and the Water Rat.

My Home: *The Hobbit*

Aim

1. To practise descriptive writing.
2. To use adjectives accurately.
3. To develop listening skills.

The Hobbit by J. R. R. Tolkien

Chapter one – An unexpected party

In a hole in the ground there lived a hobbit. Not a nasty, dirty, wet hole, filled with the ends of worms and an oozy smell, nor yet a dry, bare, sandy hole with nothing in it to sit down on or to eat: it was a hobbit-hole, and that means comfort.

It had a perfectly round door like a porthole, painted green, with a shiny yellow brass knob in the exact middle. The door opened onto a tube-shaped hall like a tunnel: a very comfortable tunnel without smoke, with panelled walls, and floors tiled and carpeted, provided with polished chairs, and lots and lots of pegs for hats and coats – the hobbit was fond of visitors. The tunnel wound on and on, going fairly but not quite straight into the side of the hill – The Hill, as all the people for many miles round called it – and many little round doors opened out of it, first on one side and then on another. No going upstairs for the hobbit: bedrooms, bathrooms, cellars, pantries (lots of these), wardrobes (he had whole rooms devoted to clothes), kitchens, dining rooms, all were on the same floor, and indeed on the same passage. The best rooms were all on the left-hand side (going in), for these were the only ones to have windows, deep-set round windows looking over his garden, and meadows beyond, sloping down to the river.

Notes for teachers

Read the extract out loud a couple of times. Before reading the second time ask students to close their eyes and try to picture the scene in their minds.

Assignment

1. Draw a picture of the place where the hobbit lives.
2. Discuss which details you found particularly interesting.
3. What does the description of his home tell you about the hobbit?
4. Imagine standing outside your home. Describe what you would see. Try to pick out details. Include personal comments, thoughts or asides that may occur to you.
5. Read your piece to someone else. Ask them to draw a picture based on your description.
6. People's homes can reveal clues as to the characters that live there. Think about what your description may tell others about you and your family? Ask a partner this question. Do you agree with their observations?

Notes for teachers

In *The Hobbit* the description of the front door is precise. One could easily visualise standing there and knocking at that door before entering. Once inside we can picture in our minds the decoration and could probably find our way around without having to be shown. When writing a description of your own home describe the entrance and lay out in the same way.

In the extract the narrator describes the immediate vicinity and the views from the windows. It important to include the area outside your home as this helps to set the scene and give context. If it is a road or a lane think about the type – is it cobbled, rutted, a cul-de-sac, etc? Choose your adjectives carefully and try to be accurate.

A Point of View: Treasure Island

Aim

1. To widen vocabulary.
2. To study how character is revealed.
3. To practise writing from a different point of view.

When we first start to write we automatically do so from our own point of view: our thoughts, opinions and imagination stem from our own perceptions of life. These perceptions are based on our own personal experience and because of this they are unique.

The following exercises encourage us to look at things from another point of view. In other words, to see through the eyes of someone who has had very different experiences from our own.

Treasure Island by Robert Louis Stevenson

The main character is a boy called Jim Hawkins. We see events through his eyes: Jim is the narrator and therefore the pronoun 'I' is used (this is called 'first person').

Chapter one – The Old Sea-dog at the "Admiral Benbow"

Squire Trelawney, Dr. Livesey, and the rest of these gentleman having asked me to write down the whole particulars about Treasure Island, from the beginning to the end, keeping nothing back but the bearings of the island, and that only because there is still **treasure not yet lifted,** I take up my pen in the year of grace 17__ and go back to the time when my father kept the 'Admiral Benbow' inn, and the brown old seaman with the **sabre** cut first took up his lodging under our roof.

I remember him as if it were yesterday, as he came plodding to the inn door, his sea-chest following him in a **hand-barrow** – a tall, strong, heavy, nut-brown man, his tarry pigtail falling over the shoulder of his soiled blue coat, his hands ragged and scarred, with black, broken nails, and the sabre cut across one cheek, a dirty, livid white. I remember him looking round the **cove** and whistling to himself as he did so, and then breaking out in that old sea-song that he sang so often afterwards:

"Fifteen men on the dead man's chest –

Yo-ho-ho, and a bottle of rum!"

in the high, old tottering voice that seemed to have been tuned and broken at the **capstan bars.** Then he rapped on the door with a bit of stick like a **handspike** that he carried, and when my father appeared, called roughly for a glass of rum. This, when it was brought to him, he drank slowly, like a connoisseur, lingering on the taste and still looking about him at the cliffs and up at our signboard.

"This is a handy cove," says he at length; "and a pleasant sitty-ated **grog-shop.** Much company, mate?"

My father told him no, very little company, the more was the pity.

"Well then," said he, "this is the berth for me. Here you, matey," he cried to the man who trundled the barrow; "bring up alongside and help up my chest. I'll stay here a bit," he continued. "I'm a plain man; rum and bacon and eggs is what I want, and that head up there for to watch ships off. What you mought call me? You mought call me captain. Oh I see what you're at – there;" and he threw down three or four gold pieces on the threshold. "You can tell me when I've worked through that," says he, looking as fierce as a commander.

And, indeed, bad as his clothes were, and coarsely as he spoke, he had none of the appearance of a man who sailed before the mast, but seemed like a mate or skipper, accustomed to be obeyed or to strike. The man who came with the barrow told us the mail had set him down the morning before at 'The Royal George' – that he had inquired what inns there were along the coast, and hearing ours well spoken of, I suppose, and described as lonely, had chosen it from the others for his place of residence. And that was all we could learn of our guest.

He was a very silent man by custom. All day he hung round the cove, or upon the cliffs, with a brass telescope; all evening he sat in a corner of the parlour next the fire, and drank rum and water very strong. Mostly he would not speak when spoken to, only looked up sudden and fierce, and blow through his nose like a fog-horn; and we and the people who came about our house soon learned to let him be. Every day, when he came back from his stroll he would ask if any seafaring men had gone by along the road. At first we thought it was the want of company of his own kind that made him ask this question, but at last we began to see he was desirous to avoid them. When a seaman did put up at the 'Admiral Benbow' (as now and then some did, making by the coast road for Bristol), he would look in at him through the curtained door before he entered the parlour; and he was always sure to be as silent as a mouse when any such was present. For me, at least, there was no secret about the matter, for I was, in a way, a **sharer in his alarms**. He had taken me aside one day, and promised me a silver fourpenny on the first of every month if I would only keep my "weather-eye open for a seafaring man with one leg," and let him know the moment he appeared. Often enough, when the first of the month came round, and I applied to him for my wage, he would only blow through his nose at me, and stare me down, but before the week was out he was sure to think better of it, bring me my fourpenny piece, and repeat his orders to look out for "the seafaring man with one leg."

How that personage haunted my dreams, I need scarcely tell you. On stormy nights, when the wind shook the four corners of the house, and the surf roared along the cove and up the cliffs, I would see him in a thousand forms, and with a thousand diabolical expressions. Now the leg would be cut off at the knee, now at the hip; now he was a monstrous kind of a creature who had never had but the one leg, and that in the middle of his body. To see him leap and run and pursue me over hedge and ditch was the worst of nightmares. And altogether I paid pretty dear for my monthly fourpenny piece, in the shape of these **abominable fancies**.

But though I was so terrified by the idea of the seafaring man with one leg, I was far less afraid of the captain himself than anybody else who knew him. There were nights when he took a deal more rum and water than his head would carry; and then he would sometimes sit and sing his wicked, old, wild sea-songs; minding nobody; but sometimes he would call for glasses round, and force all the trembling company to listen to his stories or bear a chorus to his singing. Often I have heard the house shaking with "Yo-ho-ho, and a bottle of rum," – all the neighbours joining in for dear life, with the fear of death upon them, and each singing louder than the other, to avoid remark. For in these fits he was the most over-riding companion ever known; he would slap his hand on the table for silence all round; he would fly up in a passion of anger at a question, or sometimes because none was put, and so he judged the company was not following his story. Nor would he allow anyone to leave the inn till he had drunk himself sleepy and reeled off to bed.

His stories were what frightened people worst of all. Dreadful stories they were – about hanging, and walking the plank, and storms at sea, and the **Dry Tortugas**, and wild deeds and places on the Spanish Main. By his own account he must have lived his life among some of the wickedest men that God ever allowed upon the sea, and the language upon which he told these stories shocked our plain country people almost as much as the crimes that he described. My father was always saying the inn would be ruined, for people would soon cease coming there to be tyrannised over and put down, and sent shivering to their beds; but I really believe his presence did us good. People were frightened at the time, but on looking back they rather liked it; it was a fine excitement in a quiet country life, and there was even a party of the younger men who pretended to admire him, calling him a "true sea-dog" and a "real old salt," and such like names, and saying there was the sort of man that made England terrible at sea.

In one way, indeed, he bade fair to ruin us, for he kept on staying week after week and at last month after month, so that all the money had been long exhausted, and still my father never plucked up the heart to insist on having more. If ever he mentioned it, the captain blew through his nose so loudly, that you might say he roared, and stared my poor father out of the room. I have seen him wringing his hands after such a rebuff, and I am sure the annoyance and the terror he lived in must have greatly **hastened his early and unhappy death**.

Assignment

1. In the extract Jim describes his first meeting with the captain who comes to stay at The Admiral Benbow Inn, which his father runs. What do we learn about Jim?

2. What details are revealed about the captain?

3. Thinking about the character of the captain re-write the beginning of *Treasure Island* from the captain's point of view. The events that occur will be similar, i.e. discovering the inn, meeting Jim and his father, solitary walks on the cliff, etc. However, the thoughts he reveals will be quite different from those of Jim's.

Write using the first person 'I'. In order to 'get under the captain's skin' it's important to invent a plausible reason as to why you (the captain) are there. You have enlisted the help of Jim who is to look out for a man with one leg. Why? You don't necessarily have to explain your reasons but this may account for the way you behave.

Reread the original passage a couple of times and make a note of any details relating to the captain that may help you to adopt the character. Imagine yourself as an actor.

Notes for teachers

Students should each be given a copy of the extract.

Vocabulary

This book was originally published in its full form in 1883 and therefore it will be useful be to establish the meaning of some phrases and vocabulary before beginning the writing exercise. Coloured highlighters could be used to pick out relevant words or phrases in the text.

- Buccaneer – pirate or sea-faring robber.
- Treasure not yet lifted – not discovered.
- Sabre – sword with curved blade.
- Sabre cut – scar.
- Hand-barrow – wheelbarrow.
- Cove – a small, sheltered bay.
- Capstan – a wooden rotating machine used on ships to pull ropes to hoist a sail. Sailors working it would often sing songs called 'shanties'.
- Handspike – a lever with wooden pole used on a ship.
- Grog-shop – a place selling alcohol.
- A sharer in his alarms – equally anxious.
- Abominable fancies – terrible dreams or imaginings.
- Dry Tortugas – Islands in Gulf of Mexico.
- Hastened his early and unhappy death – brought about his death faster.

Question one

Jim has a good memory. He is asked to write down the details of Treasure Island and can; when recalling the old seaman he says, "I remember him as if it were yesterday ...". He is observant. His description of the captain is detailed: 'a tall, strong, heavy, nut-brown man, his tarry pigtail falling over the shoulder of his soiled blue coat, his hands ragged and scarred, with black, broken nails, and the sabre cut across one cheek, a dirty, livid white.' Jim has a vivid imagination. He was told by the captain to keep a look out for a 'sea-faring man with one leg.' Jim states, 'On stormy nights … I would see him in a thousand forms … Now the leg would be cut off at the knee, now at the hip; now he was a monstrous kind of a creature …'.

Question two

The captain's physical appearance.

- He is tall, strong, heavy.
- Dark skinned.
- Has a scar on one cheek.
- Coarse hands with broken fingernails.
- Hair in a tarred pigtail.
- Wears a soiled blue coat.

The captain's character

- Likes alcohol – drinks a lot of rum.
- Suspicious of visitors: 'When a seaman put up at the Admiral Benbow … he would look at him through the curtain door before he entered the parlour.'
- Has a temper: '… he would fly up in a passion of anger at a question, or sometimes because none was put.'
- Tells stories: that 'frightened people worst of all. Dreadful stories … '.

Question three

Individual accounts will differ. This is an exercise which allows students to be creative, bearing in mind the character and his situation (answers to question two will help).

Example

The Admiral Benbow looked quiet enough. There was a good view of the cliffs and the cove below. This could be the place to stop. I banged on the door. Inside I called for a glass of rum and eased myself into a chair by the fire. I spied a young boy watching from the doorway. He could be useful ...

Acknowledgements and Permissions

We are grateful to the following for permission to reproduce copyright material:

The poem "I am a Pack of Cards" by Isabella Benfield. Reproduced with kind permission; The poem "What is Red?" by Mary Devenport O'Neill, published in *Prometheus and other poems*, Jonathan Cape, 1929; The poems "I am a Pencil" and "Ode to a Dining Room" by George Godfrey. Reproduced with kind permission; The poem "Autumn" by Brian C. Kelley, copyright © 2017. Reproduced with kind permission of Brian Kelley, www.theteachersguide.com; An extract regarding 'The adventurer Grizzly Griller' by Winston Kelsey. Reproduced with kind permission; An extract from *The Lion, The Witch and the Wardrobe* by C. S. Lewis, copyright © C. S. Lewis Pte. Ltd. 1950. Extract reprinted by permission; The poem "What is Gold?" by Miia Lord. Reproduced with kind permission; The poem "Christmas" by Milly Parker. Reproduced with kind permission; An extract from *The Hobbit* by J. R. R. Tolkien, copyright © The Tolkien Estate Limited, 1937, 1951, 1966, 1978, 1995. Reprinted by permission of HarperCollins Publishers Ltd; and an extract regarding 'Year 6' by Alex White. Reproduced with kind permission.

In some instances we have been unable to trace the owners of copyright material, and we would appreciate any information that would enable us to do so.